When the Shadow danced with the Light

When the Shadow danced with the Light copyright © 2017 by Maddy Saleem. All rights reserved. No part of this book may be used or reproduced in any manner whatsoever without written permission except in the context of reviews.

Illustrations and cover design by Maddy Saleem.

When the Shadow danced with the Light

For my high school English teacher, who shone the light on my writing and helped me grow in confidence.

Without your help, this book would not have been published.

Contents

The Changing Flower............................8

Sins..10

The Woman Of Your Dreams...............11

A Storm..12

Tragedy..14

Heartbroken......................................15

Object..16

The Last Goodbye.............................17

Awaiting Your Spirit...........................19

Glass Rose..20

Her Heart..22

Nature Is Disturbed............................24

Meet Me Where The Sky Touches The Sea..25

Yes..28

Pieces..31

When the Shadow danced with the Light

Starry Eyes..32

His Star..33

Protected...34

Fairyland..35

Night Beauty..36

Pain..37

Rainbows...38

Full Moon...39

For The Love Of Death..............................41

The Hidden Light.......................................42

Liar...48

Lost Elijah, My Elijah Lost..........................51

Celestial..54

A Grey World...55

   Patience..57

   The Dead Rose..................................58

Mother...60

A Graveyard Of Stars............................63

Be Happy...64

Go...66

Tears..69

The Girl Who Sleeps With Wolves............70

Fear...71

A Fallen Star..72

Nobody Knows.....................................73

Her Majesty..74

Death Of The Night...............................76

Dorian..77

A Plastic Memory..................................80

Ask..82

The Changing Flower

When Spring awoke,
she blossomed to life
as a Tulip,
all innocent and bright.

When Summer came,
under the warm sun,
she grew into a Daisy,
smiling sweetly at everyone.

Autumn fell,
and her soul was full of adventure.
A vibrant Dahlia, she was,
dancing her way through to December.

Winter arrived;
she sharpened into a Rose.
Her colour contrasted with the heavenly white beneath-
the blood red petals turned black as they froze.

When the Shadow danced with the Light

Sins

He was
left
with tremendous pain,
when all humanity abandoned his soul.
It stabbed at his heart,
laughing like the diabolic wind,
prickling his skin,
as the Demon danced
on the surface of his brain.

The Woman Of Your Dreams

If you follow her,
to the depth of the bleak forest,
your immoral soul
will blacken,
like the intentions she hides
under her demonic smile.

When you sleep with her,
under the beautiful yet
hellish
blanket of night,
her unholy secrets will
drive out your feeble
heart
and sicken it.

As you drink her darkness
that subdues you,
and relish the taste
of her malice,
do not break when you feel the
sinister scorch
of the departure of
your mortality.

A Storm

Where are the doors, in this overpowering   Hell?
The Storm in my head imprisons
my thoughts, clouding the
vision of death. I cannot
focus; the turbulence
is confusing, whilst
the ashes of my
confidence
is blinding;
flying around
me, mocking
my state.
I will never
find the
doors,
to
escape
this
infinite
Hell.

When the Shadow danced with the Light

Tragedy

She was the Moon;
a prodigious enchantress.
The florescent light she radiated,
spread warmth and contentment
over all who worshipped her.
But,
she was a tragic beauty;
when the flame of the sun arrived,
she faded,
and died.
Her holy soul,
was remembered every night.
A goddess she was,
shining her luminous light,
so bright.

Heartbroken

The Sparrow's
heart remained whole-
fixed with its elegant content.
The Crow must not have stolen her happiness
after all;
tucking her smiles and her laughter
under his wing,
when he flew
away.
For she still had her soul-
the glowing light inside her,
that would always
value more,
and shine brighter
than the Crow's
whole existence.

The Pianist

The tide washed over me,
as his fingers caressed the keys;
I was underwater,
floating between the waves
as his calming melody
soothed me, and
cleared all thoughts from my mind.
He wouldn't let me drown-
the rhythm that he created,
flowing gently,
kept me afloat.
How powerful this music was,
making Neptune seem so
frail.

The Last Goodbye

She sat under her tree,
every day,
breaking out in a cry.
Never wishing
for the moment,
when it would cease to live,
and die.

She held onto its aging branches,
as the wicked wind shook the tree,
howling with laughter,
witnessing the tree's misery.

She cursed the wind,
feeing the leaves fall from so high,
and lay at the roots of her tree,
fearful of the last goodbye.

When the Shadow danced with the Light

Awaiting Your Spirit

I should move on,
but I cannot.
I do not sleep at night-
I wait for the arrival of your ghost,
just so that I can see
your face
one last time.

Glass Rose

You may call me a Glass Rose.
Because if you break me,
I will cut you-
my petals will flourish with colour
as they absorb the warmth of
your blood.

When the Shadow danced with the Light

Her Heart

I once saw an old lady, sat alone,
cradling her heart against her chest.
Its beat was heavy, exhausted and slow
as it struggled for warmth between her breasts.

I asked her why she held her heart so tight.
And she responded sorely with a sigh.
She stroked her heart faster with misery,
tears falling, so I watched her wondering why.

Her fingers clutched it tightly and hard
as her wary eyes wandered around.
Her heart began to cry with a terrible sound.
"Oh why?" she cried. "Don't die!"

When the Shadow danced with the Light

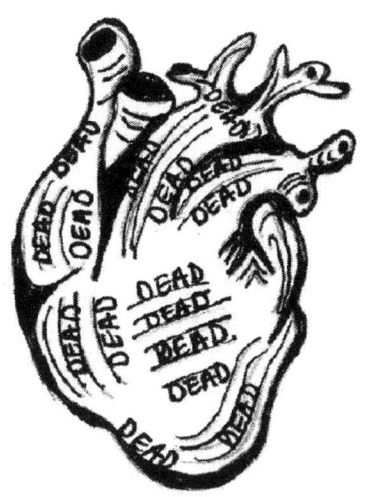

Nature Is Disturbed

The trees shook in terror,
and the wind screamed sharply;
watching the sun fade,
as the night murdered her.

When the Shadow danced with the Light

Meet Me Where The Sky Touches The Sea

Have you ever heard
about the love between the Sky and the Sea?
The Sea reflects the Sky's emotions
so that she knows she's not alone.
How joyful the Sea is,
when the Sky is blue.
How miserable the Sea is
when the Sky is dull. It pulls
at my heart
to know that such a love,
an illumination in my soul,
will never come my way.
Today

Tonight.

Tomorrow.

Perhaps I need to
wait

and watch how the Sky carefully kisses the Sea.
Feel the warmth of their souls as they glide their
soft
fingertips against each other's.
Listen to how the Sky giggles and how the Sea
roars
deeply in return-
with no sense of worry.
Think about their love,

Their perfect relationship.
They are right,
they belong,
for eternity and
beyond.
No matter how much fight, at night,
even in sleep
when both are vulnerable and weak,
they keep each other safe.
Till this day
they are perfect.
They are exquisite.
So,
if you want a love like this-
find me.

Meet me
where the sky touches the sea.

When the Shadow danced with the Light

Yes

Slipping into the deep end,
she disdains the reflection underneath her.
Like the tide taking one's soul away,
the picture ripples and then floats away.
The many fragments of her body,
slides smoothly along the sea.
Breached.
Bitten.
Bruised -
like the ocean parting.
Her damaged heart crumbles into ash
as her neck touches the surface of the water.
The bitter taste of tears lingers on her lips.
Fresh.
Pure.
Clear-
the air taking its last turn to try and rescue her.
In over her head
as she catches one last breath
she
sinks.

Cold blue liquid covers her timid self-
innocence in the depths of Neptune's waters.
Fearful flashbacks enclose around her-
a siren seducing a small fry.
Her brown eyes stare
as her three terrors swim by,
leading her to Hell's gate.

When the Shadow danced with the Light

A hand to her throat,
filled with the same blood as hers.
Instead of a kiss,
a stick grazed her cheek.
He never called her "dear".
The beastly eyes always overlooked her in disgust.
All he would ever ask for was
a beer.
A section of her heart cracked as she replied,
"Yes".

Chains pulled her through and pinned her to the desk.
Eyes everywhere.
Noise everywhere.
Her skin burned-
sweat dripping down her as the demonic laughter entered her ears,
echoing as if she were stuck in a cave,
where nobody could hear,
Her eyes watered as she focused on the teacher's voice.
A call to her name as her heart cracked again.
"Yes".

The boy in her English class-
an angel living in those dull dungeons.
His blue eyes lightened up her soul
every time they blinked.
But her sorrows crept in,
darkening her soul once again.
She just didn't belong.
As her feet quietly shuffled past him,

his voice calmed the air.
The one her heart longed for.
"Are you okay?" he would ask.
Her heart shattered completely.
"Yes".

She wants to be free.
Being accepted is what she wants.
So,
as her isolated body floats to the surface,
her mouth outstretches into a smile.
This,
is what she wants.
She takes her

last

breath

and

whispers,
"Yes".

Pieces

She abandoned me,
and left only a jigsaw puzzle.
Every day,
I tried to put the pieces together,
but the most important parts
were missing.
I could not find the soft and delicate
hands that fit mine,
or the radiant and stunning smile
that prompted the one that belonged to me.
The puzzle remained incomplete,
without her.
Our memories
would never
be
whole
again.

Celestial eyes

Your eyes held
the universe;
so beautiful and wonderful.
Perhaps,
that is why I got lost in them,
and couldn't find my way out.

His Star

He lived in a beautiful galaxy,
surrounded by heavenly stars.
Yet he only stared at
her.

Protected

Do not grieve for me,
for now I am free.
My soul belongs to almighty God.
There is no safer place for me.

Fairyland

I live in a beautiful land,
Where Daisies and Lilies scatter the ground.
And between them, lay pixies,
sleeping peacefully, safe and sound.

Around me, fly fairies,
dancing gracefully in the air.
Their fluttering wings burst a spring of colour,
blossoming like the flowers in their hair.

In the heart of it all, lies a fresh green Lagoon,
with elegant mermaids swimming,
under the shining, bright moon.

Night Beauty

Beautiful things happen at night time:
the sun goes to sleep,
the moon awakens.
His enlightened soul fades into emptiness-
the darkened sky snatches him away,
steals him forever.
How does the sun love the moon so much?
His death is swift, but bleak.
Their children come out to play-the little stars
commemorate the light
that shone from the sun-
miniscule beads of luster:
a bundle of brilliant gems.
all innocent and beautiful.
The beauty of the moon shines over the warmth
inherited from the sun,
her wonderful family.

Life is still beautiful,
even when covered by darkness.

Pain

This is to you,
my pain.

My heart fills with exultation,
pumps it through the snakes that wire my insides,
when a needle touches my skin.

My bones break out in laughter,
vibrating through my nerves,
when my insides shatter from
within.

My stomach grumbles with yearning,
boiling the acid in my centre,
as blood
escapes
my soul.

But of all those,
the pain that I long for the most,
the one that's dear to my life,
is The Love that you give me-
when I cannot hurt myself
no more.

Rainbows

I knew that I was the sun
but
I was too lost in our rainbow,
to notice that
you
were the tears
of the sky.

Full Moon

If you want to love me,
learn to love me like the moon.
For I am a wolf-
each night I cry,
for a love, I yearn to touch.

For The Love Of Death

She fell in love with his ghost-
every night he would visit her,
with the most pleasant company.
There was something about Death,
that she found so exquisite.
She was deeply in love.
He made her feel
so alive.

The Hidden Light

I raise my hands in front of my face,
and cup my palms slightly.
My heart is filled with content and peace.
I inhale a gentle gulp of air.
And call on

My protector,
before I listened to you,
I was nothing.
My worthless soul was always asleep
and my eyes never opened.
My bed wasn't comfortable:
it was a rotten fruit
waiting for the predators to crawl around it,
devour it.
I despised it.
At night,
the sinister wind would cackle at me and steal
my
only comfort-
leaving me with nothing but the pavement, so
hard and cold.
I sometimes heard a voice, so intimate and
well known to my heart,
calling a familiar name.
But when I looked up, it wasn't her.
And the child with the same name,
wasn't me.

When the Shadow danced with the Light

One peculiar night caused a spontaneous
dream.
A vision,
with the feeling of unsettlement lingering
in the air.
Was I dead?
Perhaps I was already in my grave?
The dense ambience,
complete silence,
created an uneasy consciousness
that boiled in my throat.
My soul lurched forward
ready to
fall.
But then a bright light shone before my eyes,
causing me to stumble back.
It radiated from the sky.
My thoughts traveled far and wide;
was it the moon?
Or was it just the stars that shared their power
to create such an illumination?
But this was not like any other light-
this had stopped me from falling.
It had been sent here to cease my death.
No force of nature was powerful enough to
create something so pure.
No being was strong enough to conjure
something
so mighty.

When the sun awakened,
I did too.

My Creator,
you opened my eyes to an unfamiliar sound;

mellow but full of light.
It protected me
and the voice that recited the words soothed
my darkened soul.
I could hear the joy of laughter,
I could see the radiance of happiness and
peace.
It was almost as if paradise was there,
overwhelming my eyes with its lustre,
glow and brilliance.
My heart was wild until it absorbed all of this
glory.
Now it was tame. I was to blame
for all the darkness in my past life.

But now
my heart longed for something other than want
and despair.
What I truly needed was
the religion that I have come back to.
The beauty
that God- the most kind and true
has gifted all of us.

I was lost in the heart of peace.
All shame and ignorance were pulled from me
as the ways of my leader comforted my body
and guided me down the right path.
Peace be upon him.
The Messenger.
My bright soul smiled, wishing I could see his
face and thank him for his guidance.
Oh, what a heavenly sound it was!
The water that was once acid
but now pure,

When the Shadow danced with the Light

streamed down my face as my mind
echoed the rhythm.
The words captivated me,
calling upon my heart, so warm and free.
You were calling me.

And I listened to you.
For the first time in my life,
peace and tranquility followed me
everywhere.
You are the most merciful.
Please forgive me for not hearing you before.
You have paired me with my soulmate
and our children were a gift from you.
But most of all,
my heart is filled with serenity and comfort.
Let the light blind you,
so that you won't forget that God is with you.
Thank you, my Lord.
Thank you for everything you have done for me.
I will never forget you.
Thank you,
for showing me the light.

Ameen.

Maddy Saleem

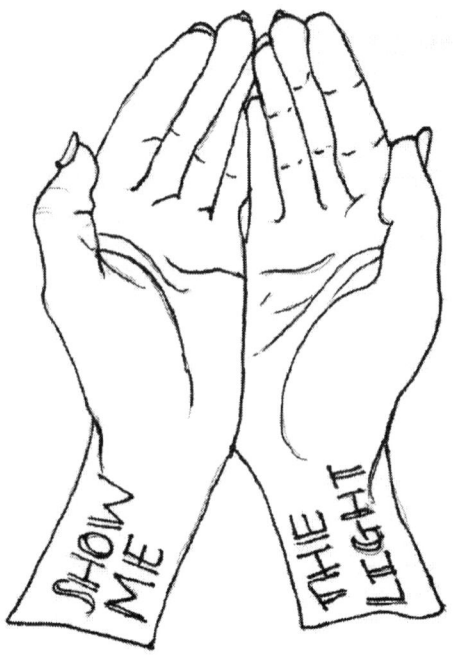

Liar

Don't you cry,
for the tears that you
shed,
are made of glass.
They hurt,
destroy
and pain
those who you push past,
leaving them to bleed on the doorstep,
like you left me.
So,
please do not let those drops of acid
roll,
down your face,
convincing me that you are still whole.
Do not try to manipulate me again.
Don't cry those fake tears,
and perceive them as clean and holy,
like the falls you promised to take me to,
when you took interest in the purity of nature.
Stop pretending,
excepting humanity to welcome you back in an
embrace-
you ran from us.
To your own selfish life,
you chased.
Your sadness isn't real,
you cannot lie anymore.
Your tears are made of glass;
Alas,
I can see right
through them.

When the Shadow danced with the Light

Lost Elijah. My Elijah, Lost.

Where are you Elijah?
I cannot find you.
The muscles in my legs are weakening-
my arms too.
It's ok Elijah.
I won't stop running.
I will find you-
of course, I will.
Oh,
my
Elijah.

I thought we would be together,
till the end of time.
You are standing there,
waiting for me at the end of the light.
Forever and always Elijah-
you promised me.
I cannot find you Elijah.
I need you.

Elijah, please.
Come out from where you're hiding.
Like how we used to play in the woodlands;
you hide,
I come and find you.
Oh, my Elijah, remember!
I would always find you.
And I always will.

Maddy Saleem

I will never see you again,
despite my hope of us
being together in the afterlife.
A sense of joy to my heart at the thought of us together.
In paradise.
Alone.
Just us.
Peace.
Nobody else.
Me and you.
my,
Elijah.

I still cannot find you Elijah.
It cannot be.
I died for you-
a concept I still cannot fathom.
My eyes closed and your eyes watered.
I don't understand Elijah.

It was real. I swear it.
Everything I did was for you.
But it seemed as the blade ripped through my heart,
yours brightened.
Why Elijah?
I was always the key to your heart.
Wasn't I?
I will always love you Elijah.
And you will always love me.

Hark! I can see you.

When the Shadow danced with the Light

I will watch over you,
as I am doing now-
witnessing my blood on your hands and the relief
pour
out of your soul.
Despite what you've done,
I will never take my eyes off you Elijah.
You're not dead.
I am.
Your beloved.
I have found you Elijah.
Always and forever.

You are lost Elijah.
my Elijah,
lost.

Celestial

She was an exquisite galaxy;
the stardust in her hair,
glowed brightly,
as she walked though the
starlight.
When she smiled,
she held the moon in her eyes,
shining sensitively,
comforting my mind.

A Grey World

At dawn,
I long to witness
the greyness of the sky
washed away by the bright sea:
a blue so satisfying,
it ripples through my mind and
as I breathe I'm floating between
the waves.

I wish to see
a sunrise so warming,
bubbling with the colours of
a volcano.
The vibrancy of the elements
will no doubt boil through my fingers
down to my toes,
waking me with the calmest feeling,
as they flow gently through the sky.

When the sun sets,
I yearn for the scent of sweetness,
as the clouds turn pink and purple,
only to be surrounded by the citrus
of the orange and yellow.

It would be a treat,
something short and sweet,
exciting me for the next day.

At night,

when everything is packed away and
covered by the jewels of the dark,
I dream of this cycle of beauty.
I dream that one day,
I will see it.
And the power of this magnificence
will
pull
me
from the grey misery
that shelters me.

Patience

Be patient
through this journey of hardship
and struggle.

Ignore the mess,
the stress and
the disgrace your world may be in.

Ask your Lord-
pray that the day you stand before
Him,
is the most beautiful day of
your life.

The Dead Rose

He said that I was a rose,
I looked like one.
Smelt like one.
Felt like one.
But I was difficult
to keep alive.
So, in the end,
he left me to
die.

When the Shadow danced with the Light

Mother

You are precious,
wonderful,
beautiful.
Everybody wants someone like you,
to cradle them as they suck.
To let your strong,
proud fingers stroke their hair when they feel
down. Around
the world, everybody has one.
But you,
are special.
You are the jewel that I will take care of forever.
A diamond you are,
sacred.
I thank God for letting me have you.
You are perfect-
no other human has
Paradise under their feet.
Just you.

So, I look at you with respect and honour,
and I pray for you.
I pray to God,
"please grant her the highest rank in Heaven".
Your light shines as a mother,
daughter and
wife.
Everything you do is for
us.
Your family.
So, I wish,

When the Shadow danced with the Light

I pray,
I cry
for your elegant wings to fly to that special place
that rests beneath you.
Every step you take,
every clench you make, with your toes,
it is there.
Right there.
And I pray you get it.
I pray to God with all my heart
because I love you.
I've loved you
from when I kicked you from inside your womb.
I've loved you since you fed me and not
yourself.
I've loved you through the hard times.
But I will never,
for as long as God lets me live,
let go of you.
My fingers will always be there to clasp yours.
My lips will always be there to kiss your cheek.
My prayers will never stop leaving my mouth.

You are my life.
My soul.
You are everything,
that I want to be.
You are precious.

You are my mother.

A Graveyard Of Stars

Her mind was a
graveyard of stars;
So damaged
yet so stunning.

Be Happy

When she witnessed
the rain,
her eyes filled with
happiness
and mirrored the nature,
so pure and sane.

She danced alone,
to the rock and soul,
that filled her room
and brought her joy.

Her nails were always painted
black or white,
with rings on every one of her pale
fingers.

She laughed,
when the other "pretty" girls,
insulted her.
Her heart always danced with delight,
when she stuck her ringed fingers up,
in a rude manner,
showing off her black and white nails.
They cried,
like the rain she
enjoyed
to watch.

Maddy Saleem

Go

Leave me.
Let me be.
There is a reason I pull the
Night Sky over my head-
a reason I cannot speak
out loud.
All that you must know,
is that you must
go.

Stop being a star,
a constant jewel of the Night.
Stop trying to shine your way through
this dark blanket I hold over me.
Leave me

alone.

Stop being the moon,
so strong and bold,
thinking you can get under my blindness,
and somehow hold me close to you,
sharing your burning pride.
I will not take your warmth.

I don't want you.
I don't want your light.
I just want myself.

Maddy Saleem

I just want to be alone.

Just

Me.

Me and my Night.

When the Shadow danced with the Light

Tears

The tears that
fall
from my dear eyes,
are more precious than those
that are blind.

The tears that
pour
straight down my face,
hold mighty awe
of this wonderful place.

And as I pray
for God's mercy,
my cries are heard from the place,
I wish to see.

The Girl That Sleeps With Wolves

Do not provoke me.
For I am the girl that sleeps with wolves.
Don't treat me like a pet
because I shall attack with my pack
and make you my prey.

Fear

Fear her;
she smiles at the sight of
fire.
She laughs at the sight of
blood.
She has been through hell and back.
And she will not go through it
again.

A Fallen Star

You are a star wrapped in skin.
No force of nature can darken the
light you hold
within.

Your perfection illuminates through the
darkness that clouds your life-
without darkness, there would be
no light.

You are elegant in everything you do.
The secrets hidden underneath you are
of something pure
and true,

When a star
falls,
it sparks an element of surprise and envy.

You are a star-
the most beautiful thing on this desolate
ground.
You are a star wrapped in skin.
Forever holding beauty
within.

Maddy Saleem

Nobody Knows

Loneliness was my friend,
and it knew my secret;
I missed you.

When the Shadow danced with the Light

Her Majesty

Her crown consisted of jewels,
that were unique to her in every way;
engraved in the base of her crown,
were stretchmarks,
that curved in a way that rainbows
would if they were just
as beautiful.

The centre of her crown
was filled with wondrous
specks of acne,
that glistened like the miniscule stars of the night,
waving at those,
who stared back
at them.

On the tip of the sacred crown,
wrinkles and blackheads
crept forward in guard,
protecting it from those who desired
to steal the worshiped
piece of royalty.

Maddy Saleem

Death Of The Night

The star fell,
and on the
ground it bled,
staining the earth with its
upmost beauty.

The moon cried,
vanishing into
the heat that
it overlooked.

Till this day,
the clear and perfect
beauty
remember the fallen.
The infant stars
twinkle in hope and commemoration
whilst the wolf
sings the song of death,
under the wailing moon.

Maddy Saleem

Dorian

When Dorian died,
the world was
a continuous night.

The memories
roll
down my cheeks
as I weep,
remembering his
beautiful face.

His eyes,
as crystal as glaciers,
glowed a vibrant blue
enlightening my soul
and those
around him.

At night,
In the dark, dim
surroundings
he was the best comfort.
My hand often lay upon
his gentle chest,
And it was the best;
listening to his subtle breath,
feeling the rise and fall
of his delicate heart.

His warmth always radiated,
and soothed my nerves.
On some nights,

When the Shadow danced with the Light

I hated,
when he decided not to sleep
next to me.
For even on those irrelevant,
hopeless nights,
I missed him.

Now he has gone forever,
and it feels like my
heart leapt out of my
chest and jumped
into the grave that I dug for him,
on the day that he deceased.

The funeral was calm,
and above,
the trees stood still,
remembering the great loss.
I loved him so much.
He was mine,
until he left.
I can still remember his
Innocent little paws-

black and white they were.
The touch of his fur was gentle
and the way his whiskers tickled
my hands,
still sends a rush of sadness
through me.
I still hear his timid
voice in my dreams
as I feel the empty
space on the bed
beside me.

Oh,
Dorian!
Why did
he have to go?
He has left me all alone,
to call this night that
surrounds me,

home.

A Plastic Memory

She was a porcelain doll;
eyes,
as round as the fatal moon,
which overpowered her delicate features.
Her petite and pinched nose
and her full red lips
caught his full attention
as his yearnful heart weakened.
Her skin,
broken yet so fascinatingly beautiful,
called for the touch of his fingers.
Beneath her look of innocence, she was a Siren,
dangerously drawing him closer,
to nothing.

The tears,
full of belonging and desire,
streamed down his cheeks.
He yearned to stroke back
the auburn curls which
framed her face.

Their connection was tragic;
he could not touch her,
could not have her,
despite his eager desire.

The familiar emotions
that he felt,
did not mean that she
belonged to him.

Maddy Saleem

She was a statue-
a solid figure that
would stay in his
mind.
She was terrifyingly exquisite,
like his first love-
the one who faded away.

This beauty;
a plastic memory,
was precious-
a reminder of what he
lost,
and what he would
never
have again.

When the Shadow danced with the Light

Ask

The almighty watches over you-
even in the blindness you think you can hide.
He witnesses the tears you wipe away-
the ones you believe are so transparent, no
heart can feel them.
The false smiles, the strained stretch of the mouth
you think everybody
will fall for-
he sees.
Pure deception.

He feels the fragments of your heart,
shatter like a porcelain doll,
breaking into concealed diamonds.
He feels the turning of your stomach,
as your insides pivot in terror.
You are so certain that He does not know
because
this all happens inside,
You.

He knows everything.
He feels the hunger of the flowers when they are
flaccid.
He hears the cries of the moon when the sun
wakes up.
He sees the terror that takes place on this Earth.
He created you.

So just do it.
Just ask Him.

Ask Him

To heal you.

When the Shadow danced with the Light

Even the darkest shadows, will dance in the light.

- **Maddy Saleem**

Printed in Poland
by Amazon Fulfillment
Poland Sp. z o.o., Wrocław